Cartoon Nation presents

POLITICAL PARTIES

by Michael Burgan
illustrated by Charles Barnett III

CONSULTANT:
Michael Bailey
Colonel William J. Walsh Associate Professor
of American Government
Georgetown University, Washington, D.C.

Capstone
press

Mankato, Minnesota

Graphic Library is published by Capstone Press,
151 Good Counsel Drive, P.O. Box 669, Mankato, Minnesota 56002.
www.capstonepress.com

1 2 3 4 5 6 13 12 11 10 09 08

Library of Congress Cataloging-in-Publication Data
Burgan, Michael.
    Political parties / by Michael Burgan; illustrated by Charles Barnett III.
    p. cm. — (Graphic library. Cartoon Nation)
    Summary: "In cartoon format, explains the history, role, and influence of political
parties in the United States" — Provided by publisher.
    Includes bibliographical references and index.
    ISBN-13: 978-1-4296-1334-7 (hardcover)
    ISBN-10: 1-4296-1334-3 (hardcover)
    ISBN-13: 978-1-4296-1782-6 (softcover pbk.)
    ISBN-10: 1-4296-1782-9 (softcover pbk.)
    1. Political parties — United States — Juvenile literature. I. Barnett, Charles, III, ill.
II. Title. III. Series.
JK2265.B86 2008
324.273 — dc22   2007031040

Art Director and Designer
Bob Lentz

Colorist
Michael Kelleher

Cover Artist
Kelly Brown

Editor
Christine Peterson

Editor's note: Direct quotations from primary sources are indicated by a yellow background.

A direct quotation appears on the following page:
Page 26, from a January 1940 speech given by President Franklin D. Roosevelt.

TABLE OF CONTENTS

Who doesn't like a party? You meet with friends to eat, dance, talk, and have a good time.

But not all parties are alike. In the United States, millions of voters belong to political parties. These people like the other kind of parties too. But with their political parties, they have important work to do.

Voters join parties that reflect their ideas about what's best for the country. They choose party members as **candidates** to run for office.

Candidates who win try to carry out the party's beliefs as they make laws and run the government.

Americans don't have to join parties to vote. But party members have more say in choosing **candidates** than independent voters do. And sometimes they throw great parties when their candidates win.

I guess all that hard work was worth it.

Good job!

Yea!

candidate — a person who runs for elected office

LEVELS OF GOVERNMENT

Most U.S. voters elect officials who serve in different levels of government. These officials serve at the local, state, or national level. All governments pass laws, raise money, and address the needs of citizens.

NATIONAL GOVERNMENT

STATE GOVERNMENT

LOCAL GOVERNMENT

This crowd is getting heavy, even for me.

In 1787, a group of talented American leaders met in Philadelphia at the Constitutional Convention. They created a new national government. It was stronger than the one used in the United States during and after the American Revolution (1775-1783).

Strong? Feel these muscles! Come on!

U.S. CONSTITUTION

Some people called me the Father of Our Country.

I call you heavy.

Two years later, George Washington was elected the first president of the United States.

Across the country, everyone agreed that General Washington made the perfect president. He had proven his bravery and love of the United States during the Revolution.

THE CONSTITUTION

The Constitution of 1787 outlined the form of the national government and basic U.S. laws. It called for each state to choose special electors to pick the president. The Constitution never mentioned political parties.

Political parties didn't exist for this first election. The leaders who wrote the Constitution thought parties divided people. They wanted Americans united as they built their new nation.

But not everyone liked the new government created by the Constitution. Some people thought it had powers that should belong to the states.

And some of the leaders who helped elect President Washington now argued over how to run the country.

The Constitution created a federal government. Under this system, power is shared between the national government and the states. Alexander Hamilton led the Federalists. This political group favored a strong national government.

Hamilton wanted a strong national bank and hoped to strengthen industry in the country. To carry out his ideas, Hamilton wanted a national government with more power than the states.

Opposing the Federalists were the Democratic Republicans. One of the party's leaders was Thomas Jefferson. He supported the interests of farmers, not bankers. His party wanted the states to have more power than the federal government.

As the Federalists and Democratic Republicans debated their ideas, a two-party system began. This system is still used today. Smaller parties can form, but two major parties usually compete to run the government.

Stronger national government!

More power to the states!

A new broom sweeps clean, and I'm sweeping you out.

In 1800, Jefferson was elected president. His party took power for the first time. In some government jobs, he replaced Federalists with Democratic Republicans.

THE SPOILS SYSTEM

And take this spoiled food with you.

Nobody likes food that spoils, but U.S. leaders love the spoils system. Spoils are prizes won from an enemy in battle. Political spoils are government jobs and contracts for work. A party taking power rewards its members with jobs. Today, party loyalty is not enough to get most government jobs. Laws require people to pass tests to show they have skills for the job.

9

Good Feelings?

After Jefferson's win, even more Americans supported the Democratic Republicans. Under President James Monroe, the country entered the "Era of Good Feelings," because one party was so firmly in control. With no political battles, the government seemed to run smoothly.

But Democratic Republicans didn't always agree on important issues, such as the nation's economy. In 1824, four party members ran for president.

The Electoral College

When Americans vote for president, they are actually choosing people from their state who are called electors. The electors then select the president. If no candidate has enough electoral votes, the House of Representatives chooses the president. If one party controls a state's electors, it can easily win the vote for its candidate.

The election was close and no candidate had a **majority** of the votes. The election was finally decided by the House of Representatives. John Quincy Adams won, and Andrew Jackson was second.

majority — more than half of something; a candidate needs a majority of votes to win an election.

Jackson ran against Adams again in 1828. Adams' supporters were called National Republicans, while Jackson ran for the Democratic Republicans. Jackson won and served as president until 1837.

During Jackson's presidency, parties created the first platforms. These platforms were a list of goals they hoped to reach if they won. Each goal was called a plank. Taken together, each plank built a party's political platform.

In the first U.S. elections, only white men who owned land could vote. By 1832, most white men had won the right to vote. Women, Native Americans, and African Americans, however, still could not vote.

The Democratic Republicans were now called Democrats. They worked hard to win the support of new voters. The Democrats held parades and put up posters promoting their candidates. The other parties of the day did too.

The Democrats also used a new way to choose presidential candidates. Before, party members in Congress held a meeting called a caucus to choose a candidate. In 1832, the Democrats switched to a national convention. Each state sent delegates, who chose the candidate.

Parties still use conventions to choose candidates for president. Some state parties also have conventions. Caucuses are mostly used to choose candidates for local offices.

THE DEMOCRATIC DONKEY

In 1828, opponents used a donkey to make fun of Democratic presidential candidate Andrew Jackson. The Democrats, though, thought donkeys were good, hard-working animals. Jackson used an image of a donkey on some of his posters. Years later, a cartoonist used a picture of a donkey to stand for the Democrats. Today, the donkey is still a symbol of the Democratic Party.

Democrats helped create the model for the modern U.S. political party. All party members, not just leaders, helped decide how the party was run and who the candidates would be.

Make it good, Sam, and all the parties will want to be just like me.

We'll do the dirty work.

Back then, a strong party meant candidates didn't have to be wealthy or famous to run for office. They knew other party members would help.

The winning candidates then rewarded their helpers with jobs.

And I'll take care of you now that I've won.

It's good to be in control.

In the two-party system, parties hope to win a majority in Congress so they can pass laws that reflect their concerns. Parties also try to control state and local governments to further push for their platform.

Don't get too comfortable over there.

Controlling those offices can give the ruling party in a state more influence on national politics.

I want to see red everywhere. The more red, the more Republicans in office.

PARTY PRESSES

The rise of modern parties gave new power to an old political tool: party presses. These were newspapers tied to a political party. Party presses always supported one party's views and candidates. Today, most newspapers are not tied to a certain party.

Martin Van Buren helped the Democrats develop the first national party. He worked with Andrew Jackson and became president himself in 1837.

I wish he didn't talk so long.

MARTIN VAN BUREN

In his home state of New York, Van Buren had been part of the first political "machine." This machine didn't make tools or other goods. Instead, it turned out loyal voters.

TAMMANY HALL

The Democratic Party in New York City ran the most famous political machine. The Tammany Society was a social club that later turned to politics.

Starting in the 1850s, Tammany Hall controlled city politics for almost 100 years. The most famous boss of this machine was William "Boss" Tweed. He briefly went to jail for breaking labor laws.

Political machines reached their peak after the Civil War (1861-1865).
Immigrants flocked to large cities such as New York. Machine leaders, called
bosses, helped the newcomers get jobs and become U.S. citizens. In return,
the immigrants voted for the machine's candidates.

Welcome to America,
folks. Vote right this way.

immigrant — someone who comes from one
country to live permanently in another country

Political bosses sometimes broke the law. They bribed officials
or stole money that belonged to their cities. New laws said
many public jobs had to be based on talent, not party ties.
The machines lost more power in the 1900s as the national
government took on the role of helping the poor.

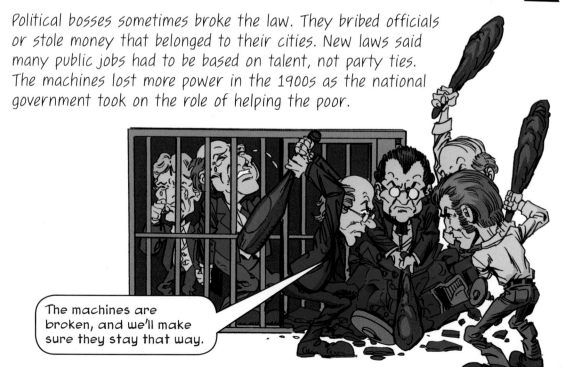

The machines are
broken, and we'll make
sure they stay that way.

HERE COME THE REPUBLICANS

By the 1850s, one issue divided Americans more than any other: slavery. Several political parties had formed to try to end slavery. Democrats also disagreed over the spread of slavery into new states.

"Hold it, mister. You stay right where you are."

WEST

In 1854, the Republican Party formed in Ripon, Wisconsin. The party's main goal was to stop the spread of slavery. The party had its greatest appeal in Northern states, where slavery was already outlawed.

THE REPUBLICAN ELEPHANT

Just as the Democrats are linked to the donkey, the Republicans have their own animal. An 1874 political cartoon showed an elephant being scared off by a donkey wearing a lion's skin. The elephant stood for the votes the Republicans usually won. Soon, the elephant came to represent the party itself.

In 1860, Abraham Lincoln was the Republican candidate for president. The Democrats were now so split that they had two candidates. Lincoln received no electoral votes in the South. But he won enough in the North to become president.

Since that election, the Republicans and the Democrats have been the two major parties in the United States. They have won all the presidential elections. One of these parties has always controlled Congress.

That man will ruin us in the South.

Why I oughta . . .

Go ahead, I dare ya!

PRESIDENTIAL SCOREBOARD

Political parties try to control the nation's top job of U.S. president. Over the years, more Republicans than Democrats have served as president.

REPUBLICANS
19

DEMOCRATS
9

We've got your party beat, Franklin.

The game's not over yet, Abe.

ABRAHAM LINCOLN

FRANKLIN D. ROOSEVELT

THREE'S A CROWD?

At times, party members might feel strongly about issues they think the leaders ignore. Politicians who feel left out can start their own parties. Or they can run on their own, with no party ties.

It's time for somebody else to get a chance.

THEODORE ROOSEVELT

Hey, Roosevelt! Who invited you?

I'm a former president. I don't need an invitation.

Smaller parties are called third parties. They've been around since the 1840s. One of the most famous was the Bull Moose Party. Republican Theodore Roosevelt had served six years as president. But in 1912, he opposed the policies of President William Howard Taft, another Republican.

Roosevelt formed the Bull Moose Party so he could run against Taft. Roosevelt finished second to the Democrat, Woodrow Wilson.

No third-party candidate has ever become president. But smaller parties have won at the state and local level.

It was a lot easier before he got into the race.

Democrats and Republicans usually remain loyal to their parties. But third parties can force major-party candidates to address new issues. And sometimes the Republicans and Democrats have to work harder when other candidates enter a race.

WRECKING THE RACE

RALPH NADER

AL GORE

GEORGE W. BUSH

Third party candidates rarely win, but they can play a part in someone else's loss. In the 2000 presidential race, Ralph Nader was the Green Party's candidate for president. In Florida, he won nearly 98,000 votes. Vice President Al Gore, a Democrat, lost Florida to Republican George W. Bush by just 537 votes. Gore and Nader had similar views on many issues. If Nader had not been in the race, Gore might have won Florida and the presidency.

CHOOSING THE CANDIDATES

Parties try to choose the best candidate possible. In most races, candidates must appeal to independents as well as party members. With a victory, the winning party has more power to pass laws and hire people for government jobs.

primary — an election in which voters choose the party candidates who will run for office

At times, more than one party member wants to run for a certain office. Special elections called **primaries** are used to choose a party's candidate. Some states also use caucuses.

Pick me!

WHO WANTS WHAT?

The Democratic and Republican parties have some clear differences on what's most important to them. In general, Republicans favor low taxes and few laws that limit businesses. Democrats think the government should do all it can to help the poor and the sick. They want a clean environment and support workers' groups called unions.

22

Some primaries are "winner-take-all" — the person with the most votes wins. In others, a candidate needs to win more than half of the votes to be elected.

Awww. I lost my marbles.

Looks like I got the most marbles.

Yeah, but you don't have more than half.

If no one gets enough votes, the top two people face each other in another election called a run-off.

On your mark, get set . . .

Every four years, Democrats and Republicans hold primaries to choose their candidates for president. Some of these primaries are open. People can vote for candidates from either party. Other primaries are closed. Party members can vote only in their own party's primary.

OPEN PRIMARY   **CLOSED PRIMARY**

Candidates for office must tell voters who they are and what they hope to do if elected.

This process is called campaigning. The candidates meet as many voters as they can to try to win their vote.

Now I know why they call shaking so many hands "pressing the flesh."

At the national level, the Republicans and Democrats spend hundreds of millions of dollars. Party members donate some of the money. Some money comes from groups that hope the party will promote their interests. The parties use the money to hire campaign workers and buy ads.

CAMPAIGN HEADQUARTERS

DONATIONS

I've been waiting for this.

The two parties also count on many volunteers. These people work hard for their party and its candidates. Most don't expect anything if their party wins. They simply want to help.

Come on, there's always room for one more.

VOTERS' EXPRESS

BUS STOP

On Election Day, some volunteers provide rides so people can easily get to the **polls**. Having plenty of money and volunteers helps the parties "get out the vote" for their candidates. Party members hope all their work will lead to a win.

polls — the place where votes are cast and recorded during an election

IN THE VOTING BOOTH

How do you spell "Washington?"

Sir, if you're casting a write-in ballot, it's best to vote for someone who's alive.

The list of a party's candidates is called its ticket. Old-time voting machines had a lever that voters could pull to choose all the candidates on the ticket. Fewer of these machines are used today. Today, people use computers to record their votes. But voting for all of a party's candidates is still called "pulling the party lever" or "voting a straight ticket."

IS THE PARTY OVER?

In 1940, President Franklin D. Roosevelt said:

The great public is interested more in government than in politics.

FRANKLIN D. ROOSEVELT

Roosevelt believed that party loyalty was fading. Fewer people voted a straight party ticket. More people didn't join parties at all. Having the best government possible was the goal of these voters.

I'm so tired of the same old parties.

PARTY FAVORS

Percentage of voters who identified themselves as Republican, Democrat, or Independent as of January 2007:

Republican	Democrat	Independent
32.1	37.5	30.3

26

Today, party loyalty is even weaker than in Roosevelt's day. Fewer voters make it to the polls. And more citizens vote as independents instead of joining a party.

But U.S. political parties still have a role to play. The party that does not control the government makes sure the other party follows the law and serves in the interest of all voters.

If not, party leaders can work to defeat the governing party and force them out of power. Many experts believe parties have helped the United States build a strong democracy.

Whew! I'm glad this party is over.

Yeah, but we'll make the next one even better.

TIME LINE

May 25, 1787 — U.S. leaders meet in Philadelphia to create the Constitution.

MAY 25, 1787

April 30, 1789 — George Washington becomes the first president of the United States.

APRIL 30, 1789

May 21, 1832 — The Democrats hold their first national conventions.

MAY 21, 1832

March 4, 1829 — Andrew Jackson becomes president and soon starts to build the Democratic Party.

MARCH 4, 1829

March 1854 — The Republican Party forms to oppose the spread of slavery.

END SLAVERY

MARCH 1854

June 1912 — Former President Theodore Roosevelt forms the Progressive "Bull Moose" Party to challenge the two major parties for the presidency.

JUNE 1912

1790s — The two-party system begins to develop, with the Federalists and the Democratic Republicans.

March 4, 1801 — Thomas Jefferson becomes president and replaces Federalists with Democratic Republicans in some government jobs.

1790S

February 2, 1825 — With no majority vote in the Electoral College, the House of Representatives chooses John Quincy Adams as president.

MARCH 4, 1801

FEBRUARY 2, 1825

January 1940 — President Franklin D. Roosevelt warns that party loyalty is fading.

November 2000 — Third-party candidate Ralph Nader acts as a "spoiler" in Florida, costing Vice President Al Gore the election there.

JANUARY 1940

NOVEMBER 2000

GLOSSARY

candidate (KAN-duh-dayt) — a person who runs for elected office

delegate (DEL-uh-guht) — a person chosen to speak and act for others

economy (ee-KAW-nuh-mee) — the ways in which a country handles its money and resources

immigrant (IM-uh-gruhnt) — someone who comes from abroad to live permanently in another country

majority (muh-JOR-uh-tee) — more than half of something; a candidate needs a majority of votes to win an election.

political machine (puh-LIT-uh-kuhl muh-SHEEN) — a small group of politicians from either the Republican or Democratic parties that controlled campaigns and elections in major U.S. cities during the early 1900s; political machines were controlled by powerful leaders called bosses.

polls (POHLS) — the place where votes are cast and recorded during an election

primary (PRYE-mair-ee) — an election in which voters choose the party candidates who will run for office

READ MORE

Giddens-White, Bryon. *National Elections and the Political Process*. Our Government. Chicago: Heinemann, 2006.

Landau, Elaine. *Friendly Foes: A Look at Political Parties*. How Government Works. Minneapolis: Lerner, 2004.

Miller, Davis Worth, and Katherine McLean Brevard. *Political Elections*. Cartoon Nation. Mankato, Minn: Capstone Press, 2008.

Payan, Gregory. *The Federalists and Anti-Federalists: How and Why Political Parties Were Formed in Young America*. Life in the New American Nation. New York: Rosen, 2004.

INTERNET SITES

FactHound offers a safe, fun way to find Internet sites related to this book. All of the sites on FactHound have been researched by our staff.

Here's how:
1. Visit *www.facthound.com*
2. Choose your grade level.
3. Type in this book ID 1429613343 for age-appropriate sites. You may also browse subjects by clicking on letters, or by clicking on pictures and words.
4. Click on the Fetch It button.

FactHound will fetch the best sites for you!

INDEX